...So, I was thinking.

Cassandra Pownell

Poems based on reflections
of the past, self-introspection,
external observations, being lost,
feeling loveand rising again.

*This book would not be possible without the love,
inspiration, and support of my amazing wife. Thank
you, Shelly Pownell, for being everything I was
always looking for, more than I ever knew I needed
and better than anything I ever imagined. Your love
is my muse. You simply are the best! All my love,
always.*

*Thank you to the friends, family, acquaintances,
strangers and mother nature for providing
inspiration in all forms.*

CONTENTS

COBWEBS

as she lays on her pillow
the veil finally breaks
a tear swells in her eye
and gently rolls down her face
in complete silence
with unsettled choices
she feels like she is surrounded
listening to all those inside voices
in the morning she wakes
to a pillow drowned by tears
wondering what really happened
ignoring the truth behind the fear
around those she once knew
she withdraws herself now
into that empty room
where feelings are not allowed
untouched for so long
now all she can feel
is the melody of a song
the pain inside
is crying to be let out
in no one she can confide
scars cover her in doubt

VALIDATION

All of your predetermination
Judgement of my situation
Believing I live in procrastination
Or intoxication from the medication

Am I such an aberration
I will not succumb to your allegations
Sit and judge in your congregation
As I drown from love dehydration

On the brink of detonation
In a state of fermentation
Do you have any inclination
Of all my hopes and aspirations

Set on a course for termination
You do not know my tribulations
Look closer for further examination
Never did I need your validation

DREAM

You are it for me
You are all I need
You are my heart and soul
You are the reason I am whole
You are happiness
You are freeing
You are an amazing human being
You are beautiful
You are light
You are simply out of site
You are my one and only true love
You are the dream I always dreamt of

SELF-DOGMA

Parishioner of the mind
Sitting in sermon
As Reverend Pain preaches
Fragmented truths uncertain

Into the farthest corners he reaches
Dogma and negativity
Self Doubt becomes doctrine
Devout in insecurity

INDIANA

Straggly green fingertips
Brush across soft ambers and whites
As a push and pull movement dips
Gentle whispers usher in the night

The quilted layer of darkness spreads
No moment left unexplored
Crickets arise and bow their heads
Natures metronome strikes a chord

In a flash and spark
Fireflies begin to dance
Illuminating the midnight dark
In a graceful melodic trance

FRAGMENTATION

A sense of what seems to be
dream like exsistence
with emotional sensitivity
some inebriating presence

A glimpse here
scented reminders there
reality augmented
a heavy cross to bare

Perception demented
loss of communication
in a reflections empty stare
living in fragmentation

RAT

Every word you say is phony
Seeding untruths in acrimony
Believing in your sanctimony
Denouncing others in testimony
Standing high in ceremony
Do you believe you are a crony?
Feeding on your own baloney
Thinking you alone are the trophy
Bound to your lies in matrimony

NIGHTMARE

Cold stone and metal walls
Etched with nefarious shapes
Scratching and crying to break free
Agonizing in the solitude of their fate

Anguish and evil echoes loud
The sound of chaos unbearable
As you begin stepping closer in fear
Now aware of a destiny so terrible

A scream starts from deep inside
Clawing its way out
Till your eyes open and senses collide
Giving reason to doubt

HYPOCRITICAL

At all times be politically correct
Giving power to others
But putting silencers on
Anyone trying to empower

Being offensive to all minorities
Roadblocks to equality
Regression of our own progression
Keeping thoughts in poverty

Hypocrite to your very fundamentals
Pushing for acts of freedom
Judging those who speak out as
Mental
Disagreeing is nothing but treason

There is no truth In loyalty
Living in a hypocritical society

<u>MUSE</u>

An incandescent
Red hot internal light
Creativity and expression
Flowing abundantly, thoughts ignite

Moved beyond
Allowing words to flow
Bold actions and colors
Like lava from a volcano

TRUE

Love is nourishment
For the heart and soul
Let me feed you love and fill you up
Should "if" lay between us
And when "forever" seems abrupt
Remember
Our love began with a kiss
A flutter inside and a decree
Infused with tenderness and bliss
Always there I give it for
Free
Let me capture the warmth
Of the sunset for you
And let it never dim
Lounge in the pool of your gaze
Where I could stay forever and
Swim
The definition of Beauty
is this life with you
Hearts embracing one another
Know that mine will always be
True

PTSD

From wind swept beaches
To the jungle marsh
Relentless sands so very harsh

They fought for freedom
And gave up futures untold
Those left behind minds controlled

Horrors unimagined block the light
Questions cloud each breathing day
Now their reality is feeling betrayed

Others cannot imagine the fight
The battle within takes a toll
Loved ones can only try to console

Downward spiral your thoughts go
Inching closer to the brink
Asking for help is harder than you
think

Brothers and sisters
On this journey bound together
Holding on to each other by a frayed
tether

ICARUS

Always trying
Pushing limits so high
Why must you fly
So close to the sun

With simple actions
Trust comes undone
All is not always
Games and fun

Hubris will be
The undoing warned of
Rapidly you'll plummet
From your ignorance above

#METOO

I see through your hypocrisy
Betrayals and indignities
Disproportionate misogyny
A downslope of society
Do you hear the violin playing
The intro to your vain failing
I have not one concern
For how your life may take a turn
Now you know how it feels
To be the one who's made to kneel
Take it away and watch you cower
Time for women to rise in power!

CROWS

A murder convenes
Before my eyes
Blackness swirling
Sounds unnerving

Reaching out on nimble limbs
Branches bend and crack
A gathering so ominous
Chills go creeping down your back

Then suddenly all is quiet
Racing away on the winds
Like some insidious riot
Silence embraces you again

FALLING

In Love,
For Love,
My Love

A prodigious word
With gentle touches so pleasant
Strength of we unbreakable
Never obsolescent

A treasured state of mind
Finds sanctuary in the heart
Nurturing the weathered soul
Always bonding, never apart

Love is bold, love is vast
It is Incomparable to all
Our future, our now, our past
Everlastingly I fall

- For my wife

ETERNAL

She steals my breath
And heart away
In passing glances
I swoon and sway

In-depth talks
We dance and play
Relish each second
Luxuriate in every day

Souls afire in passion
Flaming so bright
Heat and desire
Illuminate the night

She calls to me
Without a sound
Whispers of eternal love
Two half's now found

YOU ARE

I have a heart
You are the beat
I have a body
You are the soul
I write the poem
You are it's meaning
I exist in this world
You are my paradise
I am in love
You are the essence

WINGS

In the freedom of the sky
Goes the child's flying eye
Shinning beautifully and bright
Wings of the graceful butterfly

Gentle whispers of precious dreams
Floating freely with the breeze
Higher than the oldest trees
No need for worry to be seen

Go on and follow your dreams
Only you can paint the scene
Like bright colors of morning light
Everything is possible within your
sight

Grow up slowly day to day
Don't let innocence fade away
So one day you can proudly say
You followed your heart all the way

And like the graceful butterfly
Flying strong along with time
Then one day you will come to find
Dreams come true all the time

SEPARATE

The two feelings
Love and Hate
They always try to separate
the world and it's people

Good or bad
Which will prevail
Anything we had right
Only seemed to fail

Maybe we've been
Kidding ourselves all along
Trying to change the world
But only together can we be strong

Helping hands free
The once chained heart
Open up to see
The old ways we must part

DON'T

You know that face
You've seen it many times before
Don't let yourself be blind
Help the innocence behind the scorn

Looking oh so helpless
Only a fragile young one
Take control of the pain
Put away the smoking gun

Remember those times
Running scared into your room
Looking for an honest excuse
Only knowing what will happen soon

Don't let the aging beast
Run free with your soul
Open up your secrets to one
Let the stories be told

Don't cry inside
The shame is so real
Don't try to hide
Let them know you feel

FOR KEEPS

After laughing and singing
Dancing in the dark
We sat together under the stars
Cooling in the water
The heat between us palpable
Delirium in this abundance of love
The whisper of forever on our lips
Knowing that what we became
is a mystery
That was meant to be solved
By only these two hearts
It is everlasting
It is for keeps
It is home

GHOST TRAIN

Years of trying so hard
To find that place
But its passed you by again
Look of bewilderment on your face
Soul full of passengers
Extra baggage you brought along
Why do you try so hard
To find where you belong
Like the runaway ghost train
Screaming along at night
Heart crying out for loving arms
To wrap around you tonight
You've travelled long and hard
Oh can you see me here
You dont have to give in
Just give up the fear
Or did the American dream
Pass you by again?

IMAGINATION

As imagination runs wild
and summer turns into fall
like an infant child
I am learning to crawl

The dancing starlit sky
doesn't seem so far away
dreams are within reach
beginning each new day

Through trial and error
life is an up and down ride
once I said I didn't care
now I know it's time to try

I can see the beauty
beyond the beast in front of me
one day I'll break away
and laugh at all I used to be

YOSEMITE

Ghostly white still standing tall
Soldiers at attention
After the battle with heat and flame
Destruction beyond comprehension

Their canopy of green halos
Will grow and rise beyond
The rebirth of natural beauty
Life finds a way to respond

In the black and ash
A blanket of white covers each root
Like milk from mother nature
Her love for the earth absolute

PISCES

AT DIFFERENT TIMES
I BROKE IN TWO
IN THE BEST WAY POSSIBLE
TO CREATE BOTH OF YOU

FROM THE FIRST SITE
IT WAS UNCONDITIONAL LOVE
THE SQUEEZE OF YOUR FINGERS
THE WARMEST OF HUGS

SO PERFECT AND TRUE
SNUGGLES FIT LIKE A GLOVE
CUDDLES AND KISSES
NOTHING BETTER I CAN THINK OF

SO DIFFERENT IN LIFE
YET AT TIMES THE SAME
IN SO MANY WAYS
I AM SO PROUD I PROCLAIM

HAVING YOU BOTH WAS A GIFT
THIS LOVE LIKE NO OTHER
YOU MADE MY LIFE WHOLE
WHEN I BECAME YOUR MOTHER

~For my children Ethan and Ciara